More praise for John A. Williams and *Safari West*

John A. Williams' poems – spanning five decades – are variously passionate meditations, sensitive philosophical explorations of ideas, or history. The reader thinks deeply about these poems on family, the slave trade, freedom, racism and love. Some of the brief poems are as quick, private and funny as William Carlos Williams' "This is just to say ..." My favorite poems in *Safari West* are the inspired and striking portraits of individuals – both public and private. This volume will add a new rich dimension to the already distinguished, multidimensional career of John A. Williams.

Clarence Major

There is this special feeling you get when you snuggle under a quilt that was made by your great-grandmother, washed and cared for by your mother, passed on to you, soft, clean, sweet smelling from the days before washing machines did wash and drycleaners did pressing. There is this special feeling you get when you remember the smell of fat meat boiling in the pot waiting for the greens to come and share a smaller space. There is a feeling you get when you look back at the beauty and wonder of our people that sends apple-boiling smells to tickle your nose, that lets you know "yes" this is not my home; only my *Safari West*. And one day, you know, you'll take the next step to be on that glorious plane.

Nikki Giovanni

Safari West

Safari West

POEMS

John A. Williams

h_p

Legal deposit/Dépôt légal, Bibliothèque nationale du Québec and the National Library of Canada, 1998.

Canadian Cataloguing-in-Publication Data

Williams, John A. (John Alfred), 1925-
        Safari west: poems

ISBN 0-9699349-2-0

        I. Title

PS3573.I4495S24 1997   811'.54   C97-901010-1

Life-size head of John A. Williams by James Earl Reid, 1988
Cover photograph by Lori Williams
Book design by Raymond Beauchemin
Printed in Montreal

Hochelaga Press, 4982 Connaught Ave.
Montreal, Quebec H4V 1X3 Canada
E-mail: hochelaga@sympatico.ca

Contents

This, too, is for Lori

Genesis

... the Ancient woke and looked about
Its waking yawn a seeming shout
In all that vast and silent space
Then sadly made the human race.

Safari West

The South Atlantic clouds rode low,
blue-fringed with rain. Snake-strong
Popo Channel writhed beneath its mud-green
surface and the boatmen pointed:
Barracudas there.
Noses like secrets, mouths of red lightning,
once they devoured nations flung aft
like galley waste, screamed flights
into Popo, now quiet, now green.
Badagry, roofed with rusted tin,
walled with ancient mud, peddles a view of
its baracoons for a Nigerian pound. For two
you heft the holding irons, glide gray
through cells silent with screams and seek
relief and rage in rasping midterror.
Chains for the slow, the strong, the quick;
chains for the mothers, the young,
chains for the nations of westbound blacks.
Crouching, I reach out of it, out of the heat;
the instruments were only metal, rusted now and
hot with the silent sun that had not screamed.
I fit them to my neck, my wrists, my legs,
feeling for what I could never feel, but
knowing that feeling hides in time, I waited.
Waited to feel, wishing for pain. Waited. Wished.
Nigerians drifted through the heat, the awful heat,
their voices like music played on their smiles
and they called: Hello, America, unhinging my

place, and wondered at the black man clothed in
the West, grasping irons, eyes swinging over the island,
to the quiet, green, sea-swirled westward wake
of the Passage, eyes thundering wet missiles.
There is an old one-pounder in the village.
It stands where a missionary in the black midtide
fired the cannon to warn his flock to flee;
that Christians, swollen white with sail,
stood in the channel again. The ships rode
high, holds filled with cheap. When the sails slid
down, the people ran deep into the bush. Not
fast enough or far; the baracoons witness
the rite. I paid the pounds. We paid the pounds.
We are paying the pounds; paying the pounds for Popo.

1969

Many Thousand Gone: Version 95

Many thousand going, gone
      to the New World chained they went,
      emptied out a continent.
      By their hundreds day on day,
      in their thousands each decade.
Many thousand going, gone.

Many thousand gone and died,
      tens of thousands marched to death;
      thousands, thousands drowned down depths
      of restless sea like galley waste,
      in rushing, blue-green watery space.
Many thousand gone and died.

Many thousand vanished souls,
      count to millions, count again,
      the girls, the boys, the women and men,
      whose bones on earth in sea point west,
      to shores where live the pitiless.
Many thousand vanished souls.

Many thousand going, gone
      down hist'ry's cunning, curling chart,
      to once more play the newest part
      that others may not have played too well
      and blunder bold through one more hell,
      with mem'ry closed to evils done
      that made so many millions gone,

       in ways that cry of great contempt
       for what we say we've always meant;
       that all are equal, same and free
       in every land caressed by sea.
Many thousand going yet.

1995

Nat Turner's Profession

In eighteen hundred thirty-one,
August hot with green and red,
I then well knew the time had come
To strike – just like the Bible said.

I felt summoned for purpose great,
This August come to Southampton.
It was the time, it was the date
to take, not plead, for our freedom.

You would not give, nor could I buy
this great abundance, wide as air,
of which this proudest nation cries,
for which we black folk beg in prayer.

I gathered round my sturdy flock:
Hark, the others, pledged and bound,
and like a marsh hawk all things mocks,
flew high then low, along the ground.

Man, boy, woman, girl, luckless babe,
we smote beneath our pounding wings;
on my command we death strokes gave
and no man balked, not one man cringed.

With blade and ball we destroyed them.
The August heat was godly breath,
leading us to Jerusalem,
thinning Virginia death by death

to get more guns. Bondage is dust
without them; ownership surely with;
God speaks like guns in August,
like banging hot iron in a smith's.

Down, let you put down your weapons,
make gone the cross we're forced to bear.
You cannot keep us without guns;
you fear us so and do not dare.

Like Washington and Lafayette,
we scoured the land for liberty,
with blood like yours, as red, as wet,
but our freedom you will not see.

Freedom did come in mighty Rome
when bold Spartacus raised the fight
and fought the empire, laid it prone.
Freedom's no gift; it's seized by might.

It came with Toussaint in Haiti,
where blood ran thicker there than rum;
There's Liberty and Equality
when in blood our freedom's won!

All men whom others hold in bond
must one day know a time is near,
when they will meet their Babylon
in those with little left to fear.

In eighteen hundred thirty-one
November came more gray than gold.
Confess! Confess! The revolt's done,
fifty-five whites in graves now cold!

Freedom? Liberty? You say for you?
O, blackness brands you chained till dead,
to water draw, and wood to hew,
to hang's to be your lot instead.

You've broken and butchered the law
with your wild, black and willful hand,
shot and stabbed all the whites you saw.
Now, Nat, you're caught and free's the land.

You know, Gray, that you dream a lie.
This land's not free and that you know,
not while our bondage blinds the eye,
and your folk don't care what they sow.

My men are dead, free men enslaved
for being so, because of me;
marched deep south to the cane field grave.
Confess! You wretch, you black disease.

My warm blood cools in Nat's silence,
his stare that swears still other Nats
will ride the road to recompense
till freedom's gained at bloody last.

What further more have you to say,
to set down firm this fiendish time
so all will know your bloody days,
and those like you who snap the line?

Who visions see and think them God's,
turn upside down the laws of State,
make what is fixed seem wrong and odd,
what's firm, what's right, a thing of hate?

I have nothing more than this to say:
Nat lifts his head as in command,
at battle's pause at end of day.
True and taut his figure stands.

I feel no guilt, and do not confess
more than to the desire to be free,
to share what you yourself possess.
And that is all I will confess.

They hanged him dead but feared him yet;
they skinned him but his ghost sprang free;
in fright they cooked him down to suet
as though each piece cried "Liberty!"

In eighteen hundred thirty-one,
November nights were chilled with fear
that Nat still damns the deeds mis-done,
and ghosts himself through every year

in altered physiology,
to ramparts mount and battle lead,
to make some words realities,
that all the world must one day heed.

1995

John Brown

In towns, cities and countrysides North
good men gather guns and guts to free you,
launch a thousand sermons from pulpit and
barber chair and from the crop-heavy fields.
You are Jefferson's firebell, his just God;
Adams' earthquake and its aftershocks.
In the heaving heart of Mississippi six
white men wait to swing for the same just thing.
Old Man, you are the end of the chapter
you well punctuated with the swish of steel
and the boom of black powder on lead balls.
Thousands there were before you, and more will
follow, themselves to script new chapters on
this struggling corpus. When men can barely
recall you, they will sense your name and feel
you marching on their spines; when the glory
seems only glitter, your deeds will echo
through the world, awakening that burning
urge for freedom that we no longer
so ferociously attend. Old John Brown.
A common name with simple stops, Captain,
like freedom unadorned, a rock, just there,
nicked with age, too deep to move, embedded.
So men gather guns and guts to free you,
and in the doing know they free themselves.

1995

23

Moremi

The love I bear you lights the bluest skies'
Unchartered coves, where there the black ensues,
And stars still blink at your marvelous eyes.
What's left of beauty on the earth is you.
Your voice summons angels to earth to present
Themselves like bees who seek your sweetness there;
Flawless your form; so fine your temperament,
That poets, humbled, from their pens forswear.
Your velvet skin, so black, so quick to wound ...
A thrust, a slash, and then away the pain,
And sudden gone without a farewell sound!
Dear child, light of all life, I must explain:
Oh! Once my love, I must have been like you;
was loved, pressed close and sweetly sung to –

I think. I've seen it done; maybe I dreamed
It was done to me – what a warming thing!
No! No! The signal! They've been seen!
Listen! The bells begin their warning ring!
They come. But not before I speak what's true.
I give you love forever, and propound:
That chains begot by hate because of hue,
Which condemns our fruit until death be bound,
Stores up for the men but a bank of rage,
But we women weep for a nation lost.
I send you to the stars that rove uncaged,
And wonders uncovered by ancient hosts.

They're here! Go now my love, this moment leave!
Rejoice I must later – but first I'll grieve.
            I mourn and I rejoice.
            Ancient, I heard your voice.

1995

25

Journey Without Name

Father fled M'ssi'ippi frightened
under a huge load of hay
dressed in a starched white shirt
grown soiled from the floorboards,
blood flowering on his shoulder
from a pitchfork tine.
He sucked his pain in silence, spat straw.
He urged faster north the horse,
the North he should not have left,
and would not, never, leave again.
So the tale is told.

His sojourn south began
with Mother's journey north.
Cute with quieted eyes and
velvet voice, certified in
cleaning, cooking and baby care,
veneered with yes'ms and no ma'ams,
she left South steerage on a Seaboard
Special. North on the Overground.
She worked till wages paid off her fare;
and extras – the usual arrangement
of freedom. Thursdays off and Theda Bara.
Mother mailed money home, scrawled script
about hip-deep snow, frozen milk
and the AME Zion Church.
These shoots of Tony and Sarah Jones,

of Gorman Williams and Margaret Smallwood
of the fled and fleeing still,
forgotten or almost, bronze urns
bearing the ash of legend – well,
they met. Married. Made love
in the blacktown hovels beside the
slow-heaving Erie Canal, where
Father wore starched white shirts to work.
In the days of Applied Science he was
a Common Laborer, and proud to be.
His body was untamed by machines;
he gloried in it. So did Mother.
Glory it's good! Hallelujah!
Genes get to grow in glories;
stagnant canals smell sweet. Hard times
hate the halo of glory, but hard
times are patient. Glory's a
false flare on a dead moon.
It was not that Gorman's heirs
turned Mother out; not that
they did not love her liquid laugh
or sassy, Southern ways. She was,
simply said, homesick and swelling
with glory. Father agreed: the
train fare was gathered.
Bonneted, blown great with pride
at her bigness, she reversed flight,
went back where rattlers warmed
in the chimney's bricks, to Grampa
Joe Jones' hardscrabble farm,

half a timbered quarter section.
In due course the midwife came.
Joe Jones got the land down through
his father, Tony, who lived thirty-five
years as a slave and forty-seven
as a black man reputed to be free.
He saw twenty-one presidents come
and go and not a one helped him be
more than he was. They were all the
same to him: white and far away,
which was better than them being
white and nearby. We are not a cussin'
clan. But at eighty-two Grampa Tony
must've said, "Darn it, Lord,
bring me on home." The request was
honored. (Mother recalls at eight,
the church bell tolling to 82,
and seeing a fly buzz under the
netting over Tony's face. "Shoo fly,"
she said, "Grampa Tony don't need company.")
So the land came to Joseph. White man
heard might be oil on Joe Jones' land;
'pproached him 'bout a trade; his land
was better than Joe's. Shook hands.
Signed papers. Joe got the good,
cracker got the bad. Joe blessed greed.
Perfumed like money, oil folk poked around.
White folk got oil rigs stamped on their
eyeballs; men got to thinking of pretty women
and houses with inside plumbing,

iceboxes and cars they didn't have to crank.
Oil folk sniffed and snuffled,
ran up hills and down dales
– and found no oil in Hinds County.
Cracker traded Joe Jones back at
the end of a double-barreled shotgun
and a pen-pushing county clerk.
Mother refused to look at the rattlers.
Father'd worked his way south with
the circus: eighteen hundred miles
of shoveling horse shit, elephant
excrescence, tiger turds, gorilla
glops and other jungle dumplings.
In his starched white shirt of good
cotton. At Grampa's said they in
that soft Southern way: "Folks down here
don't wear white shirts during the week."
Father answered, "That so?" Then trouble.
No name necessary. A victim
urgently needed. One with a starched white
shirt. Only stranger in town. They
were unable even to pronounce
innocence and Father did not stay
to spell it out for them.
The sun in Sagittarius saw me
in, slid me smoothly into the
midwife's mellowed hands two
hours past the peak of night.
Did Mother scream for me or for
Father then fast in flight?

Six months there, a season's change,
she northed again cradling a tit-crazed
boy, first of her line conceived
off the land in generations recalled barely.
Where is the glory that hurries
between homes? Grampa Gorman's folks
had fled the Lower Land before
the Railroad started. Couldn't wait.
Some things don't need no organizin',
and so ran out of steam in Syracuse.
Later came Gerrit Smith, Beecher,
Old John Brown; Ward and May, Douglass
and Tubman to build depots in the
cellar of old Yates Castle, under
May Memorial amid that slithering
great nest of cold Copperheads.
Through tree-named streets the slave-catchers
crawled – up Apple, down Orange, past Birch;
around Beech, skirting Cherry, hiding in
Chestnut. Black was the hounded, slave and free.
Some of Gorman's folk slipped farther
north and some stayed surly in Syracuse.
       The North was different but indurate
       when Gorman married Margaret in thirty-eight;
       in the Lower Land Tony just turned eight.

1980

Before Electricity, 1927

Out of a quieting chaos,
a dominating dusk, there danced, delicate
as a firefly, a firespot.
(Much later I would consider
caves at Qustul, Cro-Magnon Man;
ponder Prometheus,
lightless Lascaux in lightless times.)
More golden warm than a silver cold star
this firespot moved to meet a sibilance –
a soft and magical pop!
A swelling, stronger light, then Father's shadow
seared for seconds on the overpapered wall.
The ritual: rending holes in darkness.
The ceremony: the making of light by dark
old men to moor the sun in Sagittarius.

1984

31

My Father and Ring Bologna

My father liked its ringed redness, its lying
snaked in the pan, the gas bluing under it.
He watched it with a care filled with nerves,
his thick Italian bread oleomargarined,
his brown, chipped bowl steaming scalding water,
the tea leaves sullenly sinking.
Ready now, its juices leaking redly,
his eyes gone soft, he speared it, sliced with
luxury and I read Daddy Warbucks.
My father in ash-covered bibs amid
the Great D. We shared the meat bread tea
(milk in mine) and we were happy.
There were such times.

1972

Kids

When you have helped to raise them right
They do not kill you in your sleep.
They've already done that many a night
When they were younger, the rage more deep.

1973

Boy in the South Pacific

Into my waking youth I walked
through palm groves and guns
that slaughtered and silenced
along barbed beaches
licked by Lemurian tides.
I did not know myself.
I laughed at me, my
thin black shanks and bleached-
by-coral hair, the ageless heat-
beating gait. This was a home
through which I passed but did
not know till I was gone.

1974

34

The Cool One

His back slouched and excellently casual
The Cool One, finely draped, swings practiced
Eyes disdainfully, walks apart from the
Epidemic crowds of summer New York.
Dis-and-arranged hair melt to forehead
Moist with perspiration. Black hair like
Dank, straight strings over milk-white skin
Set around stamped black brows, soft gray eyes;
And an insincere sneer crudely carved in
His mouth's edges, relaxes upon a dangling
Cigarette. The crowds, like accidental
Curtains part, and he slips through them
Gracefully, as an actor, his broad back
Coated with summer rayon, moving slowly
With indulgent grace to nowhere special.

1953

The Age of Bop

Assonance and dissonance converge
An oblique tone; strange waves carry sheer
Through shadowed hate, in somber, gleeful fear.
This is the Age of Bop.
                   The newer urge
Of life and death in this age find record
In flatted fifths and augments, delusions of dis-chord.
The Age of Bop
                     Is one more theme of search.
Bustling Bop in retreat from Baroque
Finds its own answer, free from the yoke.

1953

P

P, I'm bearing down where you have been.
You were Astarte, pomegranate proud, dear P,
surprise, a young man's swollen spectacle.
Your cool, coy wisdom, curtained eyes, gestures,
caressed no air anywhere save Sidon's;
no breaths of crème de menthe to heat the cooling
dark; no lime-scented limbs that knew their way;
no voices sounding silver in the wind.
Brown dove you were, goddess soft, I think you now.
You graduated me, gowned me in rhythms
by moonlight. Your husband stalked the aching streets.
You started – how often! – when night had aged
to gray, sighing, rushing into little
silken things. I hear you still, hastening
home to your beating, your heels cracking
against the dawn. But back you came cloaked in
lime and mint, to race the nights again, to
taunt the dawns once more, to raise a boy to man.

1981

The Balanced News Story

they seek Sakharov
with boldface headlines
and 45-second tomes

no one misses Mandela
they don't know how
to spell Robben Island.

1978

The Evening News

Here is the news:
When we come back
More after this
After these messages
Coming up
This just in: (   ).

1978

Corion Jones

Corion Jones of Carriacou
    Calabar-bred from clans long dead,
Singer of keg drums bright painted hues.
Corion clears the Carib's view
    From wind-stained hills to sunset red,
Sea-freed sun on Carriacou.
Corion Jones will drum for you
    Rhythms of Iboland yet undead,
And ask if you're an Ibo, too.
He drums atop old Morne Jaloux
    Big drummer Jones, his legs outspread
In winds that here his fathers blew.
Casting beyond this Carriacou,
    'Nansi, Shango and tribes spoon-fed,
Cargoes, corpses, captains, crews,
To finger-beat, palm-slap, knuckle-tattoo,
    For a seeker whose searches here have led
To Corion Jones of Carriacou.

1980

Tinabu Square

Tinabu Square is not a square
it's a circle, a roundabout.
Tinabu is a memorial to
a person
a rich person
a woman
a Lagos trader who sold
her people into slavery
and thereby became
a rich person
and the woman
for whom Tinabu Square,
which is not a square
but a circle, was named.

1972

There Will Come Thunder

It takes a darkening sky and winds
then darker still, still higher winds
the slash and slit of startled gold
and then, just then, the thunder rolls.

1981

Brother

Don't "brother" me
unless you be
superior
to history.

1981

Last Will

I fear carrying there
nothing
but the slight web of my life.
I wish to bring Khufu's pyramid.
Sort of.

1982

1:2.8 at F 30: Diana in Chelsea

Huntress, found you warmth in the sagittary
When night wrapped round the Empire State
Whose lights peeked in? When *All Blues*
Sweetly urged you lay aside your battered
Mirrored arrows and see the darkness and
Not the light, not the posed grotesqueries
That gathered at your secret Armageddon?

1981

Alejo's Poem

I crept up behind the sun
resting on a blue hill,
laughing down in time.

1979

In Private

Knowledgeable of myths
we create our own
seeking truth halfway.

1972

Whisperings

Who knows origins
        or if they were endings
        anathema to desired order,
if they were glorious days?

I hear tell of
        Indians timeless as tales
        speak of magnificence Back East.
Back East is a silent sea.

I hear tell of black
        men brown men white men
        meeting in grace Back East.
Back East is a silent sea.

I hear tell of brown men
        walking the waters Back East
        before Babel was built.
In a silent sea everyone is chosen.

I hear tell men came and went
        before the doomed dinosaur
        before pterodactyl flew
and knew of light as bright as death.

I hear tell of flying things
        menlike gods out of sky

menlike gods out of sea
drifting up to hide in myth.

How goes sand on mountaintops?
How goes conifer in sea deeps?

I hear these tales and dream them, kicking,
falling fast and screaming.
My wife grips my flight and guides me back.

1972

49

Omowale X

Burnt even redder by the big suns of Mecca,
East Africa and Lagos, he was leaner
With travel and cameras swung blackly round his neck
Like burnt albatrosses pecking at time.

A beard furred his chin – a softness seen in Simba –
And his eyes, heirlooms of a devil, studied me.
He aimed a whirring albatross. Upon whose screens
do I now saunter and smile, peer past his bird?

Cooling air swept the lagoon and
Fat, paint-peeling freighters crowded to dock,
Niggerheads ready, snapping ensigns from
worlds north and south, east and west, first and third.

We worried Lagos; he lovingly murmured Mecca
But our travels bent home for this was not.
The sun dipped down the shimmering sea,
Dripping gold the peaceful Palace patio.

One year past I came again to sit where
We had sat and heard the death, the Audubon.
He had said, "Here they call me Omowale
Al Haj Malcolm X. That means, brother,
       'The child returns home.' "

1966

Skin

In a certain curve of light,
south, swollen with heat,
I cup my hands above my eyes,
and these slide out along my hand.
There, caught in the cupping, my
skin sighs iridescent secrets;
greens glazed with gold; reds
unnuanced, blazes of brightness
that would be brighter still were
I blacker and could raise up ranges
of blue. I stare. I am amazed and
I am calm with my beauty. I
return to my book.

1983

Olduvai

Dig down Olduvai
digging down
digging down
in the Rift
in the heat
digging down in Africa

Through the present
dig on down
through the past
dig on down
deeper down
through history

Past the pharaohs
digging down
past the mythos
digging down
through the false books
digging down in Olduvai

In the heat
dig on down
on the slope
dig on down
deep deep down
in Africa

Dart & Broom
digging down
Louis Leaky
dig dig down
Don Johanson
digging down in Africa

Where's Mwoka?
digging down
who's Ngeneo?
digging down
where's Mukiri?
digging down in Olduvai

Here's a jawbone
dig on down
here's a headbone
dig on down
there's a footbone
buried there in Olduvai

Homo sapiens
dig dig down
Homo hablis
deeper down
Zinjanthropus
digging down in Olduvai

Australopithecus
in the heat

Kenyapithecus
way deep down
here is Lucy
you love Lucy
digging down in Africa.

1981

The Caretaker

Our land is owned by catastrophe.
Volcanoes cracked its crust
and blackened skies that now are blue.
Warm tides entombed the trilobites
in mud that mixed to limestone.

The land was sold by a farmer
to me, measured, granted, deeded
to death; dug up, picked up, then damned.
Its bound'ry is barbed in wire or
stacked with stones. I caretake this land.

How can it be this land is owned?
The timid whitetail pays no tax,
emits ebony nuggets
to say, it seems, that it is hers,
and laces trails atop the hills.

This land is owned, how can that be?
The slick red fox knows mortgage none,
nor turkey heard but seldom seen.
Blue heron fly to fish not banks,
while awesome rides the valley down.

Benignly I nurture bluebells,
Susans brown or black, pope-white buds
on apple trees; lilies and lilacs,

cool hawks that glide on silver gusts,
rainbows crannied in a sun-swept pond.

I caretake these acres, accept
their blustering blankets of snow,
ascending summer mists that free
the sun to streak the blue with gold,
the spattered fantasies of fall.

I caretake this land, incur the
seedlings of miracles to grow,
desegregate raw wild roses,
cajole with care color and scent,
to match my time as wardens will.

1983

South Worcester Mission House

Down below the maples, there
in that cluster of white fir and the stand
of golden birch, peeling old white and poor
near the beat old church on the valley floor.
The Mission House sits. Long. Empty. Silent.
In dark brown summers it smells of woodsap
seared two centuries in sun. Pine planks snap,
unused to weight. Soft with heat, nails screech
and bend. Wasps hum home to holes of mud.
A corn snake like lissomed time coils cool
in the darkest corner. Damballah bears witness.
Silent, empty, long; no echoes of song.
Heat rotting wood does strongly smell and stain
and never makes this forested darkness plain.
One God has fled this house.
Across the road in church Sal sculpts racing
cars, cranks them up the altar and pray$.
Charlotte Valley sun lights his storm-specked
stained glass. He sips Scotch among his art
and pisses where once the pulpit stood; the
space is bathroom vaulted high, where outside
hawks wheel slow blue dreams against the sky.
When the mountains were higher, the nation
newer, Christians prayed in Sal's old church.

They'd built the Mission House. "Even one
slave, this girl," said they, "is owed

a worship place. Join her, those who care;
do guide her dusky soul to a Christian ease,
not here, but over there, among the white fir trees."

1982

Santiago Harbor, January 24, 1983

They arrived down here.
The passage must have been short compared
to the endless present they would endure.
And they must have looked up (for from the
sea all is upward) with eyes unused to sun;
gazed up Calle Heredia (not yet so-named;
they preceded him, his sonnets in the French;
he was yet to burst from between their loins);
peered up to see the framework of the church
they would finish for a God not theirs,
a God who had ironed their ankles and
shriveled their souls. Across the calming bay
they saw the Sierra Maestra into which some
would flee like shadows in the billowed bosom,
be born again as cimmarons breeding
revolts and revenges; stared up and saw
the sun and sky, so much the same they'd known
before this iron and wooden death, saw it
had tracked them, like a friendly Khoisan.
They gathered their chains and started up.

Miami Red

He hums
and smiles at The Dawn.
Superbowl Sunday. His
smile widens. He hums.
Through hip-looking shades
he studies The Dawn. Dawn
rising. Dawn coming. She is
partner, bound in black
and silver-badged. He hums.
Sees The Dawn in the cool,
new day, rising above him or
sinking like a brown sun below,
in a coop as the ocean laps
with stiff, curled tongue
along a length of silk-smooth beach.
He hums.
His radio spits like sleet. He
strokes out his 9mm piece.
A small roar rips up the street
colored a kiss-my-ass red. Atop,
racing the echo: more red and
a curl of leathered black.
He hums,
toe-dances into the street.
The Dawn watches. He knows she
watches. He humming (the beat
is Mambo), now gliding lean and black

to the white dashes middling
the sun-softened tar.
The red roar snatches his hum,
pierces his Mambo. He bends, fronts
the red blur. Squeezes.
God spits.
The red helmet bursts redly apart.
A watermelon shattered in space.
Gulls scream in fright. The red
bike is a wound in flight. The
black curl whipsnaps, spiderwebs
the windshield of a skidding car.
He hums
in the quick-frozen silence and
struts to the reddening road and
hums once more.

1989

The Men Are Crying

She told of the man who'd come to her
between night's end and day's beginning.
He was, some said, a brilliant young writer
hurrying on his career, though some
also remarked that he liked to throw
women out of windows and did not wait
to see if they bounced back up.
They sat, clock ticking in the empty spaces.
She listened, tuned to tragedy that had
rammed into the rest of her own life at
95 mph on a straight long stretch.
(No one now stirred in the other bedroom.)
He talked of his fear and of the "major
assignment" – it meant much to his career.
But as much as his life? It wasn't his
nature, those sidewalks, the double-armed
bopping walk, the rumbles, the killings.
What should he do? Good God, what must he be
to capture that from which he'd fled but yesterday?
He held his life too dear, his art too pure.
Yet the editor demanded the story be done,
yes, the rumbles; yes, the killings,
High Noons in Harlems.
The writer was fearful and he cried
there in the cusp between cornfields, and
the beautiful lady with the thin shoulders
and the night-crashed memory poured him

coffee and bourbon and never once pat
his Afro-ed head. She gracefully received
his misery and did not ever write of it.
Neither did he. He became a great success,
forgot that night and double-crossed her.

1981

A Stone for Marty Scheiner

The stone was cast into the sea
    Only the Ancient beheld the hole it made
Silt and slugs embraced it * Sun caressed it * Life arose
    Around it.

1992

The Way It Is

Give me wood and high-growth grass
        I'll build homes
Give me bags of groundnuts
        I'll build pyramids
Give me all the oil drums
        I'll give you the singing of sun
Give me your somber God
        I'll make Him want to dance
Give me old pipes
        I'll make shotguns
Give me shattered tires
        I'll make sandals
Give me virgin forests
        I'll build Monticellos.

1993

Teaneck, NJ

Our houses are rigged with all these wires;
warnings label windows and litter the lawns.
Light beams and sensors define our space.
Sirens and signals secure us in our cars.

At night the streets are speckled white; our
houses sit in cones of light. Shadows
are strangers. The power companies prosper:
kilowatts for killing fear, day at night.

The town reaps annual fees and
records systems; surcharges
for frequent false alarms. Crime pays.
It's life, these programmed protectors.

Yet once I slept with opened doors and windows
wide, summers, even on a first-floor porch.
That was before the war. But when did it
start, when will it end and who will win it?

1993

Close

My arms grasp tight their body,
protect it from the tiger
that softly stalks our dream.

1997

Walking the Wire

Barely begun we slide to its end,
flexing wire-walkers, Flying Wallendas,
poles precisely held in the gut of winds,
glissading slightly down the curve. Balance
is being. The distance down is death,
and we have done our pirouettes.

Slide-by-glide down the slender stretch we ride
the dipping nadir, two as one, one as
two in a pas de deux, twinly compassed,
feel the sinister rise and then the fall,
like our own heartbeats. It is the side-sway,
sudden as a misplaced ski, we can't make.

Now up, this thinnest wire linked to our feet
like a limb – hold it! – but not too long:
gravity has a powerful attraction,
likes all things quite properly placed.
We must see ourselves arrived there and safe,
the one like the tick before midnight,
the other like the tick at, symmetried beside.

1993

A June in L.A.

Across the stroke-sheeted bed
I stare at the graveyard beyond
the Avenue of Champions where two
fresh mounds of earth, so red, so freshly
turned, seem to be waiting.
Cypress, palm and fir trees sway, beckoning,
beckoning. I grip her hand and hold her back.
Her weary eyes beg release. Don't want
me to want to stay, she seems to say, or
maybe I hear her think. Mother cannot
see the opened graves.

1987

Willis Passing

Funerals now more frequent than
Fests of weddings, births of clan;
"Amazing Grace" and "What a Friend"
Echo plainly what had been.

In chapels, temples, churches calm,
Where each in vain serve soothing balm.
Wounded, weak, we bend to mourn
For they whose lives seem sudden shorn.

We are things in others' books;
We're scents, sounds, the way of looks,
The talks, the smiles, the way we were
When we with life did once concur.

These are previews, often come,
Garlanding him is homage home,
When we ourselves find last repose
On satin folds with powdered nose.

Now who can know the nightly dead
From bullets, beatings, lack of bread,
Of our world but badly bent,
For them who hymns with self-intent?

Who runs the rhymes of William Blake
For victims of their States' mistakes?

Resist we do, this view not ours
With no embalming, no sad flowers.

There's a subtle merging here
Of image real and rite so clear,
With distanced death, no song, no prayer,
Just dead in midstride, just not there.

Frequent now the endings run,
Friends and strangers by death done,
Sounds and silence grace their ends,
And so do we, when death commends.

1993

Flights

Milliseconds in black
they skim up a thermal in the sky,
great air-gripping wings
of Hawk, talons clutched tight.
Ripped mother Robin pursues,
shrieking, for her chick.
Diving down a draft behind,
Hawk 2 extends claws to stab her
to silence in a spray of feathers.

1994

Sea Creature

I circle you like a shark.
Yesterday I was a dolphin.
Tomorrow I will be an orc.
Next week a barracuda, who knows?
I leap up past you, a flying fish.
I ripple round you, a sea snake
(or a great strand of sea weed).
I won't bite – unless you do.
These waters are dark and deep;
they require sure swimming and
avoidance of quirky currents.
Like the mythic heavens there are
seven of these seas. Are we still
in only one?

1994

Replicatus

Consider:
the measureless reach of it,
the searing brilliance immense
without bound, the raging demonium
that attends this grandeur,
and the breeding of balances
infinite beyond reckoning
that make visible the plan
we now without wonder behold;

our scoping the skies studded
with myths and huge, shimmering gods,
their dogs and dippers and
wondrous silver symmetries.
I ponder the magic of motion,
of space rushed silently through
as round we soundlessly run,
a particle amid masses;

the present placements of worlds,
our centering on the splendid sun
whose power made "races" or didn't;
that nurtures the greens that grow
the air that we destroy; that which,
in myth and fact, tenders the soul,
grants it mystic layers of selves
though millions mean years distant;

the replication of parts and quarks,
and parsecs and atoms of the whole,
that we, in small, are copies of.
What else holds all in place? What will
suspends the splintering? Holds the
mighty Cepheids firm in form,
glues all things great in time and space,
gives presence to this odd, blue place?

Can the purpose of our presence be
another field of energy
to beam to space a grace to bind
our will, collected, one great mind,
in proper pace for all things here
though mixed and blind as atmosphere?
With worlds above and all around
we must be forever bound.

We are the aliens so it seems,
uncomprehending of our dreams.

1994

Facing Jura: 50 Years After

To Bill Robinson and Wendell J. Roye

The captain calls assembly
        October past the hedgerows
        the gray monumented *villes*
        the crackling biting calva
        brilliant bubbles of champagne
        bone-breaking rides eastward
        the Jura black as Toussaint
        blue-black as Toussaint
        old worn wary farmers
        their crimson-cheeked daughters
        as the world coughs in steel
        and the sky sucks up the sound.
On this powdering mottled plain
        to here regain for La Belle France
        what we have not for ourselves
        we shuffle seasoned soldiers
        into ranks hear tanks clank
        squeal clatter – Tommy-Cookers
        – eastward where Toussaint died
        betrayed by Bonaparte
        whose dragoons he devoured
        his tomb Jura not Port-au-Prince
        dress down the wavering line
        watch the trucks roll in.
Detail! Unloaddem goddamn boxes!

swaggering through the lines
cracker motherfucker
send a sniper God or a strafing ME
stick this sucker silent south
grave south eating French dirt
Start that fire o'er yonder
we gon' burn dem ballots boys
ain't votin' for FDR in my command
'cause yew doan git no goddamn vote
France or home no diff'ence see? 'Tenhut!!
Just one sniper? Just one plane?

That was the vote in forty-four
up in smoke a swirling stain
black men saving France again.

1995

I Think I Knew Another Tongue

This language does not like me.
Like the coldest air it sinks.
Still, I swoop down against it
As a hawk mistaking glass for space.

1986

Acknowledgments

With thanks to the following publications in which these poems have previously appeared: "Safari West," in *The New Black Poetry*, 1969; "Omowale X," in *Okike # 2*, 1972; "The Caretaker," in *Steppingstones*, 1984; "Journey Without Name," in *Callaloo # 21*, 1984; "Diana in Chelsea" and "Alejo's Poem," in *New Letters*, 1984; "Before Electricity 1927," in *African Americans and Europe*, 1992; "Sea Creature" and "Teaneck, NJ," in *Syracuse University Magazine*, 1995; "South Worcester Mission House," in *Journal of NJ Poets*, 1996; and "Miami Red" and "Facing Jura: Fifty Years After," in *Drumvoices 1995/96*. "Many Thousand Gone: Version 95," "Nat Turner's Profession," "John Brown" and "Moremi" are from the libretto of the opera *Vanqui*, by John A. Williams, 1996.